Michael's Many Mistakes

Michael's Many Mistakes

This book is dedicated to all of us who have made mistakes and learned from them.

Michael's Many Mistakes

Coaching or Teaching: the best of both

Some of you might be familiar with coaching and some might be new to the idea, so let's take a moment to explain some important definitions and distinctions in the way we work with children.

When coaching, we work from the assumption that the coachee has all the resources they need inside them to find the solution or answer they seek. The job of the coach is to use coaching techniques to unlock the internal wisdom of the coachee.

As we are coaching children, our approach has to include elements of teaching to introduce new concepts, skills and techniques. This creates a safe space to practice these new skills before your child uses them in real life situations. The way we do this is through stories, activities and the power of imagination.

With our books, you will find that we have carefully combined the two approaches of coaching and teaching into a powerful tool for you to use with your child.

Michael's Many Mistakes

Becoming Wise for your Size

Step 1: We Share

When you share a story together, you make a unique and special connection between the storyteller and the listener. When you share this story with your child, you are strengthening your relationship and making special memories.

Step 2: We Reflect

Once you have shared the story, it is time to reflect on the wisdom, insights, thoughts and feelings that the story has stirred up for you both.

Step 3: We Explore

In this step you will explore new ideas and concepts and consider the different perspectives of each character.

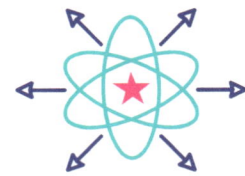

Step 4: We Experiment

You then take all this new learning and you try out these new ideas, strategies, tools and beliefs to see what works for you.

Step 5: We Prepare

If you want to develop new patterns of behaviour or new ways of thinking, it is important to plan and prepare when you will use them. Let's prepare for the next tricky time or the next opportunity!

Step 6: We Practice

The final step is to practise. Practice makes progress. Keep practising until the new learning, tools and strategies are familiar and easy to use and then you are Wise for your Size.

Michael's Many Mistakes

Step one - We Share

When we share a story together, we make a unique and special connection between the storyteller and the listener.

Our brains are wired to respond to stories in a different way from hearing an instruction or a fact. When we listen to stories, they have an amazing effect on our brains.

Listening to a story switches on several parts of our brain all at the same time; the parts we use for thinking, communicating and feeling emotions. We feel for the characters, their experiences remind us of our experiences and our imaginations allow us to explore places and situations we have not physically experienced ourselves.

Without nagging, lecturing, begging or preaching we can start to plant ideas, explore tricky topics and change perceptions simply by reading one of our coaching stories.

We invite you to begin step one. **We Share**: clear your diary for 10 minutes, switch off all distractions and electronics and get snuggled up together to share 'The Worry' and begin your child's journey to become Wise for their Size.

Michael's Many Mistakes

"Bye Michael, have a great week...and be good!"

Michael turned briefly to wave back at his dad, "Bye, Dad, see you on Friday."

Then he sped off, eager to start his week at the Hillside Adventure Camp. This was Michael's idea of fun. Five days of climbing, orienteering, kayaking, abseiling.....and no parent to tell him to have a shower. This was going to be epic!

Michael's Many Mistakes

Michael shared the Kingfisher cabin with his friends Ed, Levi and Tyler.

One of the camp leaders put her head around the door. "Hello, Kingfishers, I'm your leader, Gail. The cabin competition has begun. There is a trophy for the winning cabin, and the losers make hot chocolate for everyone on the last night. Five points for the best-kept cabin."

All four boys looked at each other and then quickly scrambled around, putting everything away neatly. The trophy was going to be theirs.

Michael's Many Mistakes

Climbing was the first activity, and Michael was a mixture of nerves and excitement.

He had never been climbing before. Halfway up, he slipped and fell. Dangling in mid-air, Michael fought the panic rising in him. Ed stood below, holding tight to the rope.

"Michael, you've got this. Just put your hands back on the wall," Ed called.

Taking a deep breath, Michael found the handhold. He began to climb again and made it to the top!

"Thanks for getting me through that, Ed."

"No problem, it's just something new. With a bit more practice, you will be flying up that tower," grinned Ed.

Michael's Many Mistakes

Back in the cabin, Tyler and Levi had found Ed's teddy, despite him hiding it at the bottom of his rucksack.

They were flinging it back and forth, just keeping it out of Ed's reach. Ed's face darkened.

"Come and get it," teased Levi. Ed lunged forward and grabbed the toy.

Michael laughed. Ed stuffed his teddy in his bag and glared at Tyler and Levi.

"Thanks for nothing, Michael," said Ed as he dived into his bunk and pulled the covers over his head.

Michael wasn't sure what to do. It's not like he'd joined in. Why was Ed so miserable? It was just a bit of fun.

Michael's Many Mistakes

The Kingfisher team was on washing-up duty that night. As Michael stacked the plates, Levi began snooping in the cupboards. "There are biscuits! Does anyone feel like a midnight feast?" Levi whispered as he snuck some packets out of the cupboard.

Michael wasn't sure. Gail had said that food cupboards were out of bounds, but I guess she would never know.

Footsteps! Someone was coming. In a panic, the boys stashed the biscuits in their trouser waistbands, covering them with their t-shirts.

That night, they feasted on custard creams. Michael thought that biscuits had never tasted so good.

Michael's Many Mistakes

The next day started with the orienteering course, and the Kingfishers were first off in the staggered start.

As they came to a clearing, they could see the next marker. They were still in the lead – for now.

"I've got a good idea," Ed grinned. "Why don't we twist this arrow marker to face down the other path? It's a dead-end, so they'll work it out, but it will slow them down."

The others thought this was a hilarious idea. They giggled as they imagined the confused faces of the other teams as they ran back and forth, trying to find the right way. It was a shame they wouldn't see it.

Michael's Many Mistakes

Laughing and breathless, the Kingfisher team made it to the finish line in record time.

"Head over to the snack table. You deserve a drink after that. The others will have to work hard to beat your time," said Gail.

Panting hard but triumphant, the team made their way across the field. "We won't need to worry about anyone beating us, lads," smirked Michael. "I took care of that."

"What do you mean?" said Ed. Michael opened his backpack. It was full of arrow markers from the orienteering course. Tyler and Levi were delighted and high-fived each other. "The trophy is in the bag for the Kingfishers," said Levi gleefully."

"You cheated?" gasped Ed.

"It's just a joke. Don't get all high and mighty now," said Michael. "You thought it was funny when you did it."

Michael's Many Mistakes

Ed was cross. "It's dangerous. The others will be lost in the forest without the trail. We need to put them back."

Michael shook his head. He was too tired to rerun the course, and he didn't want Gail to find out it was him and get into trouble.

"I'll do it myself," Ed said, and he grabbed the bag and the map, stomping off towards the tree line.

After twenty minutes had passed and no other children had finished the course, Gail and the other leaders began to get worried.

"Boys, do you know anything about this?" asked Gail.

The boys looked down and shook their heads.
Gail took off to look for the children.

Michael's Many Mistakes

Ed didn't come to the lunch hall. He was nowhere to be seen. The boys pushed their mashed potatoes back and forth but hardly ate a bite. No one felt like talking. Michael began to get a squirmy feeling in his stomach.

The leaders sat together with serious faces and hushed voices. Snippets of conversation floated over.
"Ed… arrows… cheating… shocking!"

Michael tried to enjoy kayaking, but all he could think about was Ed and how he was missing out because of something he, Michael, had done. He kept wondering how soon it would be before Gail came to tell him off.

Michael's Many Mistakes

While putting away the oars, Michael overheard Gail talking about Ed.

"Well, he didn't mention anyone else, so he must have acted on his own. I know he's no angel, but this isn't like Ed. He is in the leaders lounge thinking about what he has done."

Michael was confused. Why hadn't Ed told on him? He could have gotten out of it if he had told Gail the truth.

Heading off to the leaders lounge, Michael pushed open the door. Ed looked up from his seat.

"What do you want?" he snapped.

Michael's Many Mistakes

"I want to know why you haven't told on me yet? Why didn't you just tell Gail what really happened?"

Ed sighed, "Why didn't you?"

The fight went out of Michael immediately. He felt terrible.

Ed shook his head, "I may not always do the right thing. Yeah, I like a laugh but putting people in danger is not OK. But I did start all this. If I hadn't come up with the idea, none of this would have happened. So, I just took responsibility for my part. Admitting your part and saying sorry would be a good start."

Michael relaxed with relief, "I am sorry, Ed. I don't know why I did it in the first place. I thought it would help us win, I guess. I've felt awful ever since, but I never wanted you to get the blame for it."

Michael's Many Mistakes

Suddenly, Michael knew what he had to do. So, he headed straight to the campfire to find Gail.

It was time to tell the truth about who really cheated today.

Initially, Gail was disappointed in Michael, but he was harder on himself than she could ever have been.

She believed he was sorry for what he had done. It takes courage to admit you've made a mistake.

Gail let Michael decide how he could make amends with the others. After a campfire apology, Michael and Ed took on the washing-up duty for everyone else for the rest of the week, and they both did it in good spirits.

Michael's Many Mistakes

It was the final night and Michael was feeling mixed emotions. Overall, it had been a great week, with lots of adventures and too much dish washing. Michael had also learned to admit when he got things wrong and made up for his mistakes. He knew he would never do anything like that again so, in a way, he was proud of himself too.

The Kingfisher cabin gathered their spending money and bought the whole camp some more biscuits to pay back the ones they had taken.

"S'mores all around," shouted Michael and Ed as they sat and enjoyed the last campfire with the rest of their friends at Hillside Camp.

Michael's Many Mistakes

Step two – We Reflect

Our stories are written as opportunities to gain wisdom and insight, to learn and grow. Take some time at the end of the story to reflect on the thoughts, emotions, memories, feelings, learning, concerns and frustrations that the story has stirred.

When we are reflecting on the story, there is no right or wrong answer, no judgement of yourself or others. Listening to others reflections can also help you. To get you and your child started, here are some helpful, reflective questions:

What did the story make you feel?

When have you felt this way before?

What did the story remind you of?

What did you like about the story?

Who was your favourite character? Why was this?

Who was your least favourite character? Why was this?

What could this story teach you?

How would that help you?

What do you think happens next?

Michael's Many Mistakes

Thank you

Hello, and thank you for buying and sharing our book with your child. We hope you enjoyed reading it as much as we did writing it.

We are twin sisters who, between us, have decades of experience working with children and their parents in Health and Education. We share a passion for supporting children to reach their full potential. We have combined our knowledge, skills, and expertise to create the Wise for My Size Coaching methodology.

We are on a mission to equip and empower one million children with the mental resilience and self-confidence to live their lives without limits.

We can't achieve this alone, nor would we want to. We know that caring parents, teachers, and mentors make the best guides on the path to wisdom, so we wish to put our tools into the best hands...yours!

When not writing and coaching, you will find us usually on a dog walk enjoying the beautiful Scottish countryside.

We always love connecting with our readers, so please email us your thoughts, reactions, and wins at **hello@wiseformysize.com**.

Much love, Lorna and Jac

Michael's Many Mistakes

Wise for My Size Book Club

Did you know our brains are wired to respond to a story differently from hearing an instruction or fact? Listening to a story simultaneously switches on several parts of the brain: thinking, communication, problem-solving, and critical thinking. You can plant ideas, explore tricky topics, and change perceptions just by reading a Wise for My Size book without nagging, lecturing, or preaching.

Why not have a look at our other titles and join our monthly Book Club by visiting

www.pursuitofwisdomcoaching.com

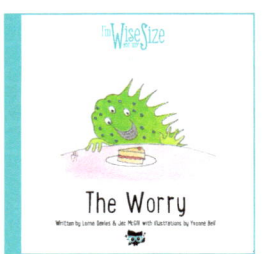
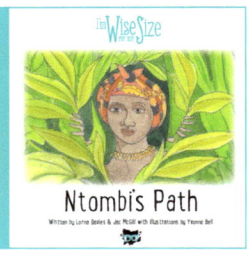
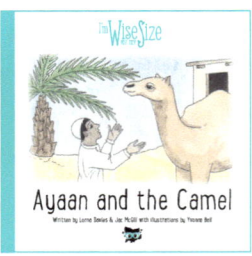
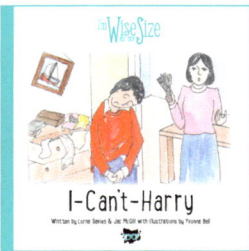
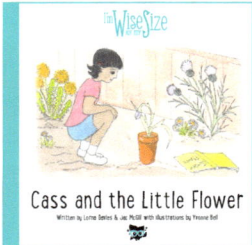
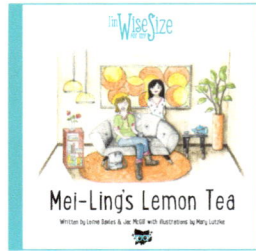
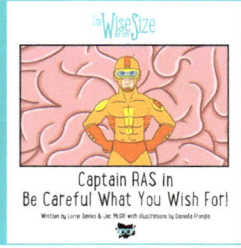
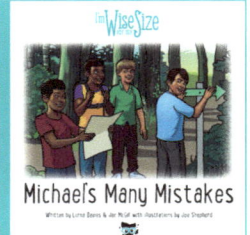

Michael's Many Mistakes

Would your child benefit from working with a Wise for My Size Coach?

Our Wise for My Size Coaches can work with your child to develop self-awareness, emotional regulation, problem-solving, decision-making, and growth mindset and build resilience, confidence, and ways to handle worry.

All our coaches have successfully completed our comprehensive training, assessment, and certification process. Please visit **www.wiseformysize.com** to find out more about our coaches and groups in your local area.

Would you like to become a Wise for My Size Coach?

The Wise for My Size Children's Life Coaching Course offers comprehensive, in-depth training packed with knowledge, practical tools, and coaching strategies through tried and tested models to aid you in unlocking children's inner wisdom and developing their self-confidence and self-esteem.

If you have ever dreamed of starting a Children's Life Coaching Business or wish to add coaching skills to your current role, please visit our website and turn this dream into a reality. **www.wiseformysize.com**

Copyright © 2022 by Lorna Davies & Jac McGill.   Illustrations © 2022 Joe Shepherd.   Graphic design by MD Creative

All rights reserved. No part of this publication may be reproduced, distributed, or transmitted in any form or by any means, including photocopying, recording, or other electronic or mechanical methods, without the prior written permission of the publisher, except in the case of brief quotations embodied in critical reviews and certain other non-commercial uses permitted by copyright law. For permission requests, write to the authors at **lorna@pursuitofwisdomcoaching.com** or **jac@pursuitofwisdomcoaching.com**

Printed in the United Kingdom by Ingram Sparks   Second edition, 2023

Michael's Many Mistakes

www.ingramcontent.com/pod-product-compliance
Lightning Source LLC
LaVergne TN
LVHW071655060526
838200LV00030B/471